RED HEART

ENDLESS PAIN

ASHMITA CHAKRABORTY

Made with ❤ on the Notion Press Platform
www.notionpress.com

Contents

Acknowledgements

This time , I thanks to my friend, who shares her feelings to me and i turn her words into a lines " i wish, i never met with you"

Feelings

since, my childhood, i heard " love is endless, it can't compare with money", Now, i hear " without money can"t buy happiness & love"

time passes & feelings changed. Its not love, love is a feeling which will not be changed for a life long.

1. I Lost To You

you break the rules and

walk in a land of ignorance.

you leave me alone and went to enjoy the beach

where a girl sitting for a long time and crying near seas.

there is no responsibility to understand yours mind

i come to seven corners and you call me again.

you will leave me but

I can't forget you,

i can't compare you,

because , i love you.

you says, i'm a golden

i smile, like a diamond,

you don't need anything

if i'm with you.

when i told you to understand me

you laugh all the times and

says " i'm nobody to you".

2. Sigh of love

im waiting for the ones
who is truly mine
even, if he is not of nines,
everytimes signs
"you are a dream"
that truly hurts.
"you are a dream "
you know this much
but, will you
be my own ?
to take care of mine.
whom i"ve never seen
but made him mine
whether he is with herself or not;
tell my heart
that you're always fine.

3. Who are You?

i came out, when the sky is clear
you smile,
when i show my seven bright colours,
Red, yellow, blue
will you give me a single clue?
i have orange, green & purple
but do not have white
im tired!
can't you give me a
piece of water bite.
i can shower you,
but you'll not like.
i have much power to change the sky
though i can't drink & eat
still i can do a try!
you admire me all times
only to know"which time is running in the clock"
when i cough , " all leaves blows , everyone thinks its a wind"
when i changed my colour to black
people's get scared and feels to get die.

4. You're the one

when i smile in happiness
you smile by seeing me,
when you cry,
i feels sad by seeing you.
i feels like you're a glue and i'm a paper
cause, we are attached with each other.
we're true,
but nave came in a single group
we do fun
but not much too
we're opposite, not know each other flew
still we're one!
to proof we're so true

5. I wish I never met with you

we were just 16th,

when we met

in a short time

you became my friends of true.

its been just a week, you became my close friend

i starts to shares my secret with you,

my friend, told me " im yours own, not he"

i didn't listened her,

its hard but for you i break my twelves years friends clue

i ignored her all the times.

i felt you're my everything,

& i fall in love with you,

i expressed my feelings to you,

you also replies, " i'm in love with you"

i was so happy that day

but i never thought that

The next morning will break my heart.

you makes my expectations avobe the sky

by saying," you're everything to me"

but next morning, you've ignored me,

and says, " who are you to me?"

you've no right to talk with me

you forget me in just 12hrs,

not only that, you also says,

go away, else i'll kill myself for being with you.

i was sad because i thought,
you're the ones who understands me,
but i was wrong
i forgot that my childhood friend was there
when no one is besides me.

6. I Never Said

I Never said -A story of a Prince & Princess-karekshpur 'Statewhichisunderthe

Rajyakushtal(king)&Bhamya(queen)andtheirdaughter

"Sunyambh"(princess)   Sukyanda'sastatewhichisunderthekushal(king)&

Brahmti(queen)theirson"karkendya"(prince). Karkendya grown,he is 5ᵗʰ

years his mother brahmti died in as sickness ;karkendya's father married

2ⁿᵈ time with bhamya's sister"Kakila" kakila seems karkendya as he

rownson. days passed karkendya gone to"Shikshaprasthan"

karkendya's Guru's name:Dhamenishwar ,kakilabirth 2 childs name

raghu and vadenshah. kakila always told to her 2childs about

karkendya. 11 karkendya is back after 10years from"Shikshasthan"

kakila,raghu,vadenshah and others were soo excited to meet the

prince. karkendya known about their 2brothers.

So,he didn't came mahal directly,(itwasafternoon)when he wentto

marke tfo rbuying gifts for his mother and brothers.

while,theprincess of karekshpur also going to visit peoples in

market(itwasafternoon)also sunyambh going to buy her new paintings

staff karkendya taken gifts for her brothers but cannot understanding

what will be the best gift fo rhis mother. (In themarket,there was no

people in the noon time as many shops get clossed).

karkendya see ssunyambh and getting close forasking "what gifts

should i take fo rmother" and sunyambh's hand carries 2plot of

paintings one is red another is yellow. 12 karkendya came close and

sunyambh turns back and the red colour falls in karkendya.

karkendya sees sunyambh and falls in love with her. Hewas
watchinginhereyes.and

sunyambhsitteddownandtryingtocatchtheyellowplot
andaftercarryingshestandsupandseeskarkendya   and
goingtoscoldhimbutshecan'tscoldbecauseshealsofell
inlove.Boththemarefallingintheireyes.

till10mintues,fullofsilenceinthatplace.afterthatthe   shopkeeperasking,
"whatyouwilltake?"   theyfastlyturned;
karkendyasays:whereareyoufrom?whatsyourname?
sunyambhsays:I'mfromkarekshpur,imsunyambh.   What'syours?
karkendyasays:I'mfromsukyandya,imkarkendya.
theysmilesateachothers.   thenagain,
karkendyasays:canyoutellmewhereshouldigiftsformy   mother?
sunyambhsays:whoseyoursmother?   karkendyasays:whyareyouasking?
sorry,butsometimesknownpeoplegetignored..   13
sunyambhunderstandsthathewillnottellabouthis   personaldetails
.so,shehelpedhimtobuygifts.   karkendyasays:wait!!
andlaughlikeanaughtyboy   sunyambhsays:whathappened?
karkendyasays: wecanbegoodfriendsright? sunyambhsays: yeah,but
itsseemsyouarenew;
karkendyasays:imnotnew,iamgoingtomymotherland
after10thyearstilltheniwaslearningstudiesin"Kendra"
sunyambhsays:okay!!anywaywewillmeetinmymahal   (home)
karkendyasays:whereisit ? sunyambhsays: Imtheprincessofthiscity.
karkendyasays:really??,bytheway,imtheprinceof   sukyanda.
sunyambh:thatsgreat,wecanbebestfriends.
karkendya:yeah,sometimesinyoursmahal,sometimes   inmymahal.
Theymeetforthefirsttime,fallinlovewitheachotherbut theydidn'tknewit!
Theyhavealongdistance. 14

sunyambh went to her home and tellshermotheraboutthe thingshappened withher inmarket. sameas karkendyameetswithhismotherandhappylyhe huggedhismotherandbrothersandtellshismotherabout thethingshappendwithhisinmarket. monthspassedandbotharefellinwitheachothermoren more. After4years,theymeet and saystoeachotherindirectly thattheyfall inlovewitheachotherandnowistomanaged theirparents. andtheymanageditwell!andmarriagedisfixed butnowtheparentshavetomeetwitheachother. Inparentsmeetings,kakilaandbhamyameets ,andthey decidedthatmarriagecanhappen. InthemarriagedayEverythingofmarriageandrituals started,andjustlefttomeetlovers.Theyaremarriednow, buttheirloveisgrowingmore. 15 but theywantedtolivealifeinavillageasapeoplenotasa princeandprincessandnotinamahal ,sotheywentto "kadurmabsi".

7. Friends are always fun

I Never said -A story of a Prince & Princess- karekshpur'Statewhichisunderthe

Rajyakushtal(king)&Bhamya(queen)andtheirdaughter

"Sunyambh"(princess)   Sukyanda'sastatewhichisunderthekushal(king)&

Brahmti(queen)theirson"karkendya"(prince). Karkendya grown,he is 5th

years his mother brahmti died in as sickness ;karkendya's father married 2nd time with bhamya's sister"Kakila" kakila seems karkendya as he rownson. days passed karkendya gone to"Shikshaprasthan" karkendya's Guru's name:Dhamenishwar ,kakilabirth 2 childs name raghu and vadenshah. kakila always told to her 2childs about karkendya. 11 karkendya is back after 10years from"Shikshasthan" kakila,raghu,vadenshah and others were soo excited to meet the prince. karkendya known about their 2brothers.

So,he didn't came mahal directly,(itwasafternoon)when he wentto marke tfo rbuying gifts for his mother and brothers.

while,theprincess of karekshpur also going to visit peoples in market(itwasafternoon)also sunyambh going to buy her new paintings staff karkendya taken gifts for her brothers but cannot understanding what will be the best gift fo rhis mother. (In themarket,there was no people in the noon time as many shops get clossed).

karkendya see ssunyambh and getting close forasking "what gifts should i take fo rmother" and sunyambh's hand carries 2plot of paintings one is red another is yellow. 12 karkendya came close and sunyambh turns back and the red colour falls in karkendya.

karkendya sees sunyambh and falls in love with her. He was watching in her eyes. and

sunyambhsitteddownandtryingtocatchtheyellowplot andaftercarryingshestandsupandseeskarkendya   and goingtoscoldhimbutshecan'tscoldbecauseshealsofell inlove.Boththemarefallingintheireyes.

till10mintues,fullofsilenceinthatplace.afterthatthe   shopkeeperasking, "whatyouwilltake?"   theyfastlyturned;

karkendyasays:whereareyoufrom?whatsyourname?

sunyambhsays:I'mfromkarekshpur,imsunyambh.   What'syours?

karkendyasays:I'mfromsukyandya,imkarkendya.

theysmilesateachothers.   thenagain,

karkendyasays:canyoutellmewhereshouldigiftsformy   mother?

sunyambhsays:whoseyoursmother?   karkendyasays:whyareyouasking?

sorry,butsometimesknownpeoplegetignored..   13

sunyambhunderstandsthathewillnottellabouthis   personaldetails .so,shehelpedhimtobuygifts.   karkendyasays:wait!!

andlaughlikeanaughtyboy   sunyambhsays:whathappened?

karkendyasays: wecanbegoodfriendsright? sunyambhsays: yeah,but itsseemsyouarenew;

karkendyasays:imnotnew,iamgoingtomymotherland after10thyearstilltheniwaslearningstudiesin"Kendra"

sunyambhsays:okay!!anywaywewillmeetinmymahal   (home)

karkendyasays:whereisit ? sunyambhsays: Imtheprincessofthiscity.

karkendyasays:really??,bytheway,imtheprinceof   sukyanda.

sunyambh:thatsgreat,wecanbebestfriends.

karkendya:yeah,sometimesinyoursmahal,sometimes   inmymahal.

Theymeetforthefirsttime,fallinlovewitheachotherbut theydidn'tknewit! Theyhavealongdistance. 14

sunyambh went to her home and tellshermotherabeutthe thingshappened withher inmarket. sameas karkendyameetswithhismotherandhappylyhe huggedhismotherandbrothersandtellshismotherabout thethingshappendwithhisinmarket. monthspassedandbotharefellinwitheachothermoren more. After4years,theymeet and saystoeachotherindirectly thattheyfall inlovewitheachotherandnowistomanaged theirparents. andtheymanageditwell!andmarriagedisfixed butnowtheparentshavetomeetwitheachother. Inparentsmeetings,kakilaandbhamyameets ,andthey decidedthatmarriagecanhappen. InthemarriagedayEverythingofmarriageandrituals started,andjustlefttomeetlovers.Theyaremarriednow, buttheirloveisgrowingmore. 15 but theywantedtolivealifeinavillageasapeoplenotasa princeandprincessandnotinamahal ,sotheywentto "kadurmabsi".